PIRATES

Pirate Perils

P Phidal

Perilously Close

It takes a keen eye for detail to be a pirate. Match your stickers to the close-ups of the dangers pirates faced on their adventures.

A Life of Danger

Rival pirates, navy ships, and rough waters were only a few of the dangers pirates encountered. Learn more about pirate perils with your stickers.

Unpopular captains faced a mutiny, which is when the crew seized control of the ship.

Captured pirates would sometimes be displayed in cages as a warning to others.

The black spot was a message of doom sent from one pirate to another.

Convicted pirates could be branded with a mark on the hand.

Pirates feared hungry sharks in the ocean, especially the gigantic great white shark.

The Kraken was a mythical monster of the deep that preyed on ships.

Pirates who came through difficult times often believed that mermaids had helped them.

Enemies would toss grappling hooks onto other ships to pull them close for boarding.

A dirk was a sharp little knife that pirates liked to use.

The word "grenade" is from the Spanish word for pomegranate, which the little bombs resembled.

A loud "boom!" from a pirate ship's cannon served as warning of a coming attack.

Captured pirates could be hanged or sent to prison for life.

Ship-to-Ship Battle

These two ships are locked in conflict, with swords clashing, cannons firing, and a hold full of treasure at stake! Finish the scene with your stickers.

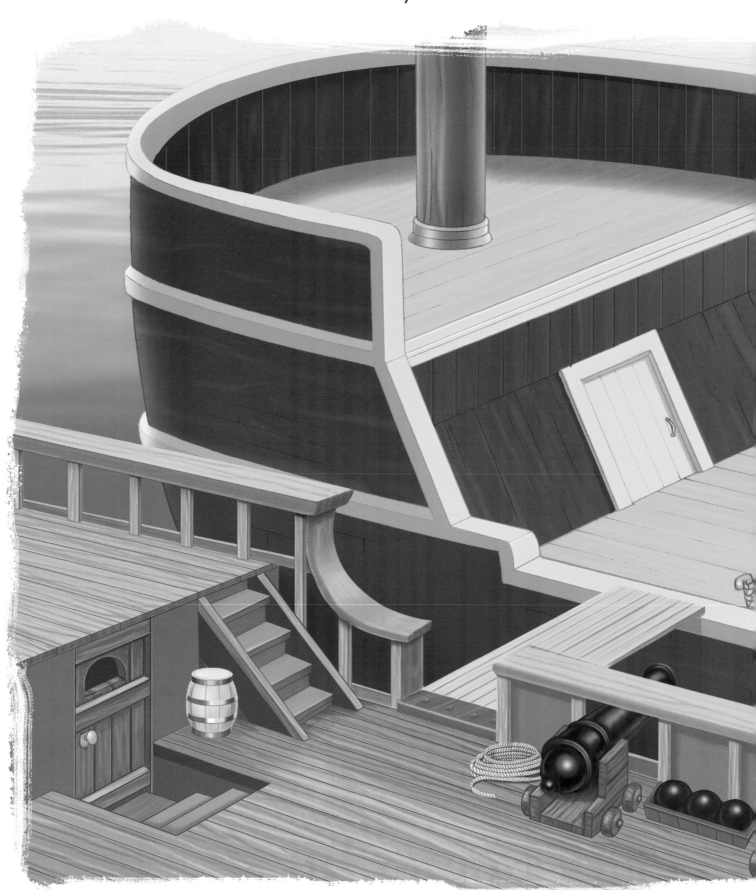

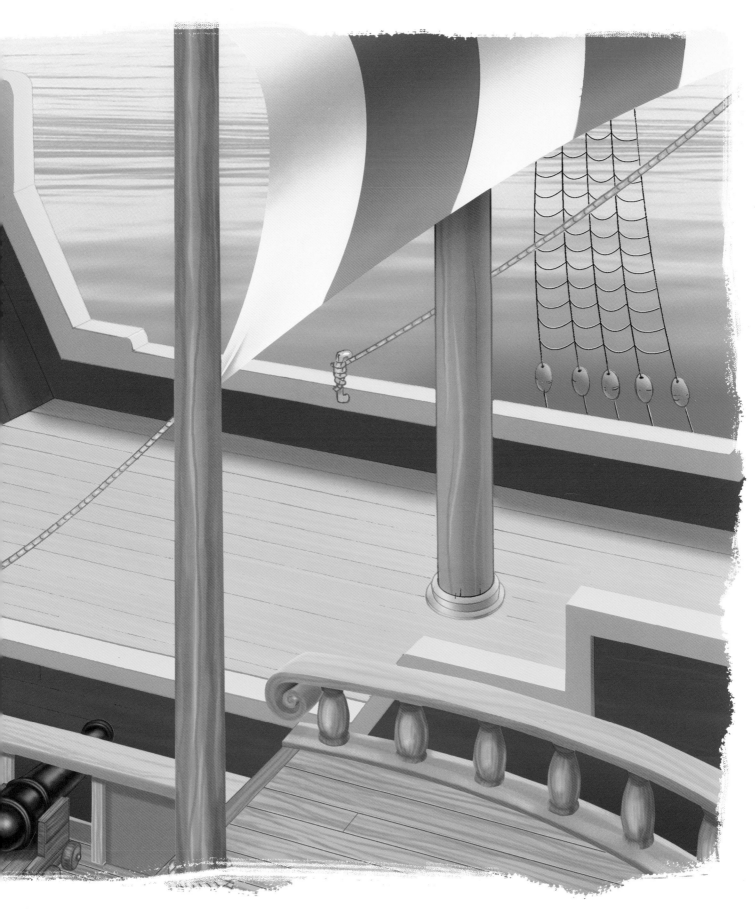

Time to Count

Pirates had to count all kinds of things, like how many miles to go until shore. Place your stickers over the shadows to get the right number.

Good Guys and Bad Guys

Though every ship had a Code of Conduct to follow, not all pirates played by the rules. Which of these pirates seem likely to live by the Code, and which do not?

Monkey See, Monkey Do

Meet a mischievous monkey who makes trouble all over the ship. The crew tries to stop him, but they just can't keep up! Match your stickers to the pranks.

The monkey steals the captain's hat.

The monkey throws the compass overboard.

The monkey takes down the Jolly Roger.

The monkey eats up all of the food.

The monkey hides in the crow's nest.

Keys, Please!

These captured pirates are being held in cages down by the docks. Help their crewmates set them free by unlocking the color code with your stickers.

Yellow + Red = Orange

Red + Blue = Purple

Blue + Yellow = Green

White + Black = Gray